W9-ALM-052

Math Monsters

ESTIMATING
How Many Gollywomples?

Based on the Math Monsters™ public television series, developed in cooperation with the National Council of Teachers of Mathematics (NCTM).

by John Burstein

Reading consultant: Susan Nations, M.Ed., author/literacy coach/consultant

Math curriculum consultants: Marti Wolfe, M.Ed., teacher/presenter; Kristi Hardi-Gilson, B.A., teacher/presenter

WEEKLY (WR) READER®
EARLY LEARNING LIBRARY

Please visit our web site at: **www.earlyliteracy.cc**
For a free color catalog describing Weekly Reader® Early Learning Library's list
of high-quality books, call 1-877-445-5824 (USA) or 1-800-387-3178 (Canada).
Weekly Reader® Early Learning Library's fax: (414) 336-0164.

Library of Congress Cataloging-in-Publication Data

Burstein, John.
    Estimating: how many gollywomples? / by John Burstein.
      p. cm. — (Math monsters)
     Summary: The four math monsters show how to estimate as they help Aunt Two Lips
figure out how many gollywomples are on her 100 trees.
    ISBN 0-8368-3808-4 (lib. bdg.)
    ISBN 0-8368-3823-8 (softcover)
    1. Estimation theory—Juvenile literature. [1. Estimation theory.] I. Title.
QA276.8.B87   2003
519.5'44—dc21
                                           2003045002

This edition first published in 2004 by
Weekly Reader® Early Learning Library
330 West Olive Street, Suite 100
Milwaukee, WI 53212 USA

Original Math Monsters™ animation: Destiny Images
Art direction, cover design, and page layout: Tammy Gruenewald
Editor: JoAnn Early Macken

Printed in the United States of America

1 2 3 4 5 6 7 8 9 07 06 05 04 03

You can enrich children's mathematical experience by working with
them as they tackle the Corner Questions in this book. Create
a special notebook for recording their mathematical ideas.

Estimation and Math

The ability to estimate is a practical necessity and an important
mathematical application. Practicing with estimation encourages
children to become more flexible about working with numbers.

Meet the Math Monsters™

ADDISON

Addison thinks
math is fun.
"I solve problems
one by one."

Mina flies
from here to there.
"I look for answers
everywhere."

MINA

MULTIPLEX

Multiplex
sure loves to laugh.
"Both my heads
have fun with math."

Split is friendly
as can be.
"If you need help,
then count on me."

SPLIT

We're glad you want to take a look
at the story in our book.

We know that as you read, you'll see
just how helpful math can be.

Let's get started. Jump right in!
Turn the page, and let's begin!

One spring day, Aunt Two Lips called Addison.

"Hello," he said. "Who can it be? Hello, hello. Please answer me."

"Hello," said Aunt Two Lips. "I am calling to ask you for help."

"I have lots of gollywomple trees in my garden. All the fruit is ripe," said Aunt Two Lips. "I want to know how many gollywomples I have on each tree. Can the Math Monsters help me find out?"

"Sure," said Addison. "We love to help our family and friends."

What are some ways that you help your family and friends?

5

The monsters went to Aunt Two Lips' garden.
"There are a lot of trees," said Mina, "and a lot of gollywomples."

"How can we find out how many gollywomples there are on each tree?" asked Split.

What do you think the monsters will do?

"I will count them all," said Multiplex.
"We will help you," said Split.

Each monster went to a tree and began to count.

"After we count all the gollywomples on each tree, we can write the number down," said Addison.

Do you think this plan will work? Will it take a short time or a long time?

9

"It is a good plan," said Mina, "but there are
so many gollywomple trees. It will take us a long,
long time."

"It will be dark soon," said Split.

"What else can we do?" asked Multiplex.

Addison looked up. He saw gollywomples in bunches. He said, "I think I know a faster way to count."

What idea do you think Addison has?

11

Addison pointed to the gollywomples. He said, "Gollywomples grow in bunches. Each bunch looks like it has five gollywomples. We can count by fives."

"Counting by fives is much faster than counting by ones," said Split.

Multiplex looked up. He began to count by fives. "Five, ten, fifteen." He saw a bunch that did not look the same. "Oh no," he said. "This will not work."

What do you think Multiplex saw?

"I see a bunch with only four gollywomples,"
said Multiplex. "That is one less than five."

"I see a bunch with six gollywomples," said Mina. "That is one more than five."

"Now what do we do?" asked Addison.

What do you think the monsters can do now?

The monsters were not sure.

"Maybe Aunt Two Lips can help," said Multiplex.
"I will call and tell her about the bunches."

Aunt Two Lips listened. She said, "Four and six are close to five. You can still use five to help you estimate."

"Estimate?" asked Multiplex. "What do you mean?"

What do you think Aunt Two Lips means when she says "estimate"?

"All the bunches of gollywomples have pretty much the same number," said Aunt Two Lips. "Some may have a few more. Some may have a few less. If you estimate, you can say each bunch has about five gollywomples."

"Thank you," said Multiplex.

"What did Aunt Two Lips say?" asked Mina.

"She said we can estimate," said Multiplex. "She does not need the exact number. A close number will do fine."

"We still must do some counting," said Split.

What do you think Split means?

"We need to count how many bunches there are on each tree in the garden," said Split.

"There are so many trees," said Multiplex. "Counting every bunch on every tree will take us forever."

"Let's estimate," said Mina. "All the trees look pretty much the same. We can count the number of bunches on a few of the trees. Then we can find a close number to estimate with."

The monsters counted about ten bunches of gollywomples on each tree.

If the monsters count by bunches, about how many gollywomples will they find on each tree?

21

Multiplex pointed to the bunches one at a time. He counted by fives. "5, 10, 15, 20, 25, 30, 35, 40, 45, 50."

"Let's tell Aunt Two Lips that we estimate there are about fifty gollywomples on each tree," said Split.

Aunt Two Lips thanked the monsters for their help.

"We are always happy to learn something new," said Addison.

Before they left the garden, the Math Monsters made up a song.

"Sometimes it is fine,
sometimes it is great
not to count but to estimate.
If you do not need
the exact amount,
you can estimate
instead of count."

Can you think of other times you can estimate instead of count?

ACTIVITIES

Page 5 Talk with children about household chores and/or community service. Ask them to think of a friend who might need help with a project.

Pages 7, 9 Take about fifty of the same small items, such as buttons, pennies, or marbles. Spread them out on a table or floor. Discuss the difficulty of knowing how many objects are in a large group when there are too many to count.

Page 11 Help children group the objects in small piles. Practice counting by fives. Let children count out fifty cents in pennies. Then use nickels. Discuss which way is faster.

Pages 13, 15 Group the objects in piles of about five. Be sure a few piles have four or six. Use this arrangement to spark discussions about the monsters' use of five as an estimate.

Pages 17, 19 Encourage children to use context clues in the story when sharing their thoughts about these questions. Critical reading is often the key to unlocking problems in mathematics.

Page 21 Encourage children to use the grouping strategy as they explore multiplication. For example, five times ten can also be thought of as five groups of ten.

Page 23 Help children understand that estimation works with all kinds of objects in many kinds of groupings. Take a walk and identify objects best suited for estimating, such as books in the library, students in the cafeteria, trees in the park, or buildings on the street.